Unlock Your Potential at Work
A Beginner's Guide to Using the Enneagram

Hillarie Kay

Copyright 2021 Hillarie Kay
All rights reserved.

No part of this publication may be reproduced, distributed, or transmitted in any form or by any means, including photocopying, recording, or other electronic or mechanical methods, without the prior written permission of the publisher, except in the case of brief quotations embodied in critical reviews and certain other noncommercial uses permitted by copyright law.

ISBN: 978-1-7361304-2-1

Published and Printed by IngramSpark in the United States of America.

Dedication

This is dedicated to the five men in my life –
each with beautiful and unique personalities of their own...

To Ben, my husband and biggest fan: I'm sure you had no idea when you introduced me to the Enneagram in 2015 this is where we would be. Your desire to know me on a soul level is what inspired this work. I'm so blessed to share this life with you and our wild crew. Thank you for always believing in me.

To my boys, Colt and Lincoln: All of this is for you. My prayer is that by watching mommy follow her dreams, you will too.

To Eric, Carter and Grant, my step-sons: You have taught me so much about myself and how important empathy is to making a combined family function. I don't always get it right, but I hope you know how much you inspire me to be a better person and keep doing this work.

Table of Contents

Introduction 11

1: The Basics 17

2: Intelligence Centers 41

3: Communication 51

4: Fighting Burnout 59

5: Time Management 67

6: Leadership 77

7: Overcoming Obstacles 87

8: Real Life, Enneagram at Work 99

Appendix 121

About the Author 123

Introduction

If you are anything like me, you've taken a variety of personality assessments at one point or another. Maybe it was Myers Briggs, StrengthsFinder, or DISC.

When I took those, each assessment provided value and insight, but I never felt they truly captured me entirely. I wanted insight into *why* I did the things that I did, not just what I did. And then I found the Enneagram.

Brought to the United States in the 1970s, the Enneagram goes beyond strengths and weaknesses. It illuminates a comprehensive look at one's internal operating system. The assessment dives deep into motivating factors, fears and core desires for life and careers. It is also unique in that it highlights the changes in one's personality during the moments of stress, in the flow of life, decision making, action taking and more.

The Enneagram is internally focused. It provides an understanding of yourself, as well as those around you.

The Enneagram helps you create more space for empathy and compassion in your actions and communication.

Improving communication with ourselves and others begins first with self-awareness of our internal operating system. Only then can we understand how it affects our external actions. I personally believe the Enneagram does the best job of this, solidifying it as a valuable tool for business and workplace development.

Before we get into the nitty gritty of how the Enneagram can help unlock your potential at work, I want to tell you a bit about myself and how the Enneagram has radically changed how I do life personally and professionally.

Why? Because I firmly believe people do business with those they know, like and trust. In order to gain your trust, I need you to get to know me and connect with me on a deeper level, rather than just the author of this book. If you don't care, and just want to get to business, I get it. Flip to Chapter 1.

Hey!

I'm Hillarie Kay, certified Enneagram coach, author and trainer.

I grew up in Central California with my mom, dad and younger sister. Both sides of my family all lived within about an hour or so of my hometown of Bakersfield. But It was clear from an early age I wouldn't stay in that box.

At 18, I got out of that box, and was one of the first in my family to move out of our region. The next phase of my life took me halfway across the country for college. I landed in Southeast Missouri. I was seen immediately with my larger than life California girl personality attempting to fit into a country culture I had no business being in.

Within 3 years I got married, hired for a position in my field of choice before I even walked across the graduation stage, graduated college, had my first son and went back to work after 3 weeks. A year and a half later, I had my second son who surprised us with a Down Syndrome diagnosis, again went back to work after 3 weeks, and all that time never stopped climbing that success ladder. By 23 I was the Director of Marketing for a medical group purchasing company, had two extra marital affairs, got divorced and unsurprisingly, was not happy or content with my life.

But boy was I burnt out.

After I was hired for the aforementioned Director of Marketing position I took a series of personality tests to see how I would fit into company culture. One of those was the Enneagram.

When I took the Enneagram assessment the first time, I was in a bad place personally, and dismissed my results. Though I didn't value it for myself, I did find it insightful when applied to the co-workers I would be with on a daily basis.

It wasn't until a year later when I was at a crossroads in my life, and was ready to finally be content, that I picked up the Enneagram again. I re-took the assessment, and as I read the results was blown away. I cried. It finally put words to feelings I had my entire life. Reading the results was the beginning of healing and direction. They helped me reconnect with myself and my purpose.

Shortly after beginning the dive into myself, I quit my job. I became a third generation business owner and opened an online full service marketing agency.

For 3 years I successfully helped business owners develop and roll out marketing strategies. But during those 3 years, I noticed a common trend that I was *not* okay with. When I left nearly every client, their marketing strategy would begin to fail and the money they invested went down with it. Why were they successful when I was implementing the strategy, but when I left, it was as if I was never there? I tried partnering with other marketing experts, only to become more frustrated with myself and my career.

I took a weekend away and had what I like to call a 'coming to Jesus' meeting with myself. I went back to my Enneagram studies with the assumption I was doing something wrong. I was right to an extent: I was building amazing marketing strategies for these clients, but I was building them for *me* and *my* personality, *not theirs*.

So I completely rebranded my business. I started using my client's Enneagram type to help build their strategies, and they worked so much freaking better.

In seeing my client's results, I realized that I wanted to do more of this type of work, ENNEAGRAM WORK! I gradually dropped the marketing side of my business, and since 2020 I have focused on the Enneagram.

I coach and train business owners, organizations and teams how to work in more sustainable ways by using the Enneagram to guide strategy and communication.

That is how this book was born. I'm going to show you why the Enneagram is the self-development tool you need to grow both personally and professionally. Let's get started.

Chapter 1

The Basics

Before you can truly get the most out of the Enneagram, there are a few things you need to know:

1. What the Enneagram Is and Isn't
2. How to Type Yourself
3. Explanation of the Diagram
4. General Overview of Type

What the Enneagram Is and Isn't

First things first: the Enneagram is *not an excuse*. One of the things I love about the Enneagram is its unique ability to help us peer into our internal operating systems, and identify the common obstacles and behaviors we may encounter in the future.

The Enneagram should be used like any other self-development tool- as information we can use to help us create sustainable strategies. We can then use those to push through common obstacles and behaviors to become better people, both personally and professionally.

It's also not something that should be used to put you in a box. I'm a firm believer that we are all unique and have our own individual path in this world. The Enneagram is a framework. If you don't agree with everything that comes out about your type, don't worry, I'm right there with you. For example, I'm an Enneagram 3 and I hate repeat *hate* working out. I highly doubt I will ever have a workout routine, but having a workout routine is almost always mentioned when it comes to those Enneagram 3 memes you see online.

Lastly, the Enneagram is not the only tool you need on your self-development journey. Although it's damn good, there is never one cure all. It's important you find other supporting tools in the journey.

However, I do strongly believe it's the self-development tool you need in your life to not only have a successful but sustainable life personally and professionally.

Now let's talk about what it is!

The Enneagram goes beyond your strengths and weaknesses, it's a comprehensive look at your internal operating system.

It is powerful! It's a personality framework based on 9 core types, and people have been using it for hundreds of years. The symbol itself can be traced back to some of the teachings of Pythagoras, the Greek philosopher who influenced people such as Plato and Aristotle.

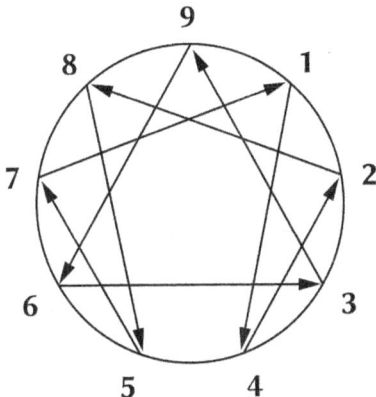

The modern version was brought to us by Claudio Naranjo in the 1970s. Though it recently resurfaced as a popular personality tool in the early 20teens.

Perhaps you picked up this book as another resource in your self-development journey, but you haven't actually taken the assessment which guides you to which Enneagram type you may be. Well buckle up for take off!

How to Type Yourself

There are a variety of free assessments out there, but if you're really serious about using the Enneagram to unlock your potential at work, I highly recommend taking the RHETI (Riso-Hudson Enneagram Typing Indicator) on

www.EnneagramInstitute.com.

Your results will come back with the top three best "type" matches. They might look something like:

> Type 3: 68%
>
> Type 8: 45%
>
> Type 4: 28%

The first type listed is not necessarily your type. The percentage numbers indicate the percentage match to that type based on how you answered the questions in the assessment.

I encourage you to read about each type listed in your top three, and hone in on what resonates with you most. You can look on Enneagram Institute for type descriptions, or keep reading this book!

If you're stuck between a couple, the first step I recommend is to look at the core motivating factors and fears of each type.

For reference, I've listed them on the next page.

Core Motivators

Type 1
Motivators: Being good, being right
Fears: Being wrong or injustice

Type 2
Motivators: Being loved, being wanted
Fears: Being unloved or not needed

Type 3
Motivators: Being valuable, being successful
Fears: Failure

Type 4
Motivators: Being Authentic, being unique
Fears: Lack of identity or significance

Type 5
Motivators: Being competent, being capable
Fears: Being helpless or incapable

Type 6
Motivators: Being secure, being safe
Fears: Lack of safety and security

Type 7
Motivators: Being satisfied, being content
Fears: Being trapped or deprived

Type 8
Motivators: Being self-governed, being independent
Fears: Being controlled

Type 9
Motivators: Being at peace, being harmonious
Fears: Loss or separation from comfort, being misunderstood

Unlock Your Potential at Work

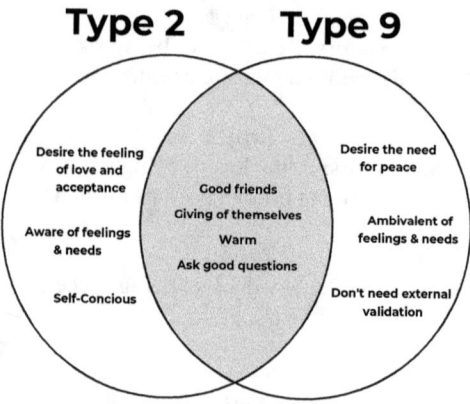

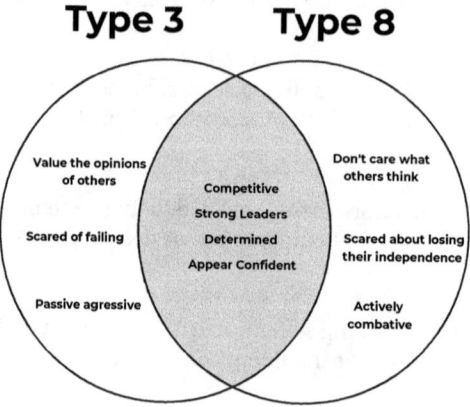

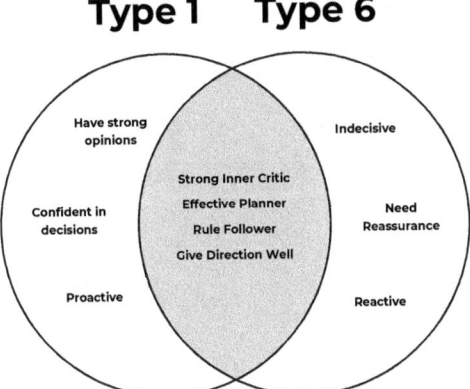

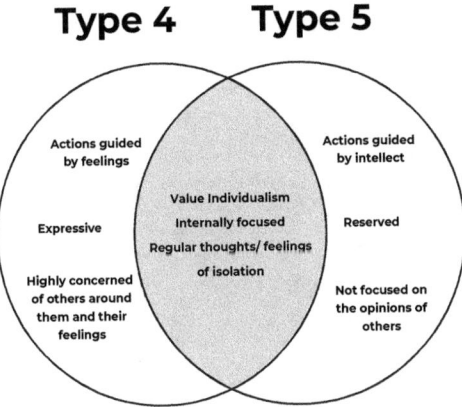

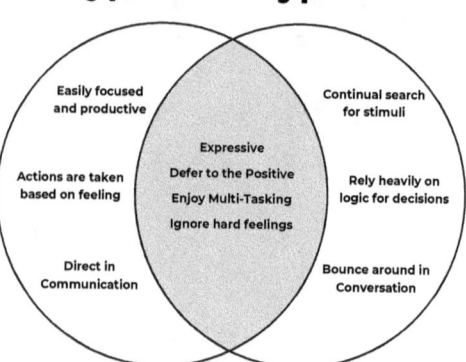

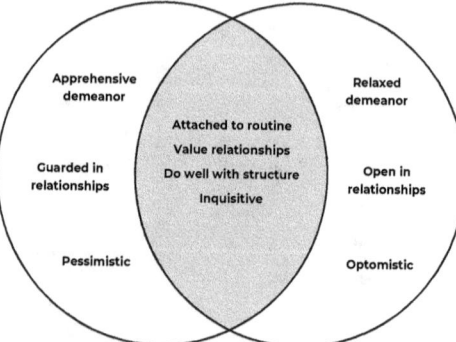

The Basics | 25

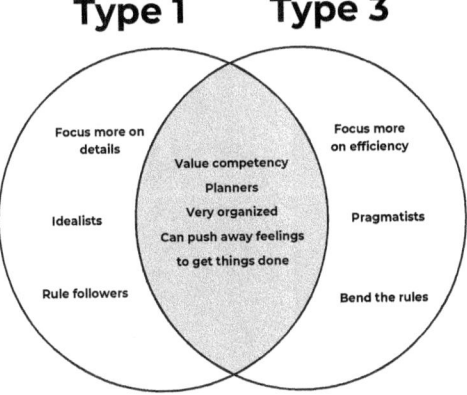

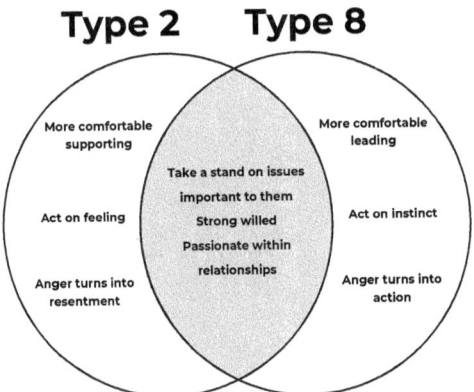

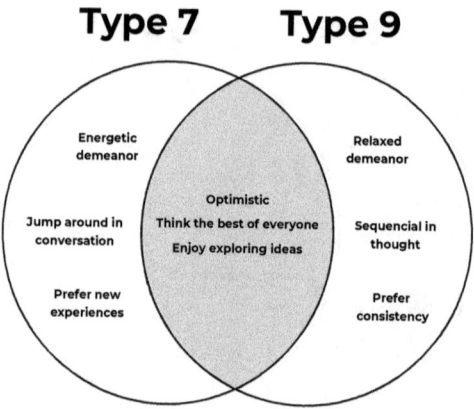

The Enneagram, just like anything in self-development, is a journey. Enjoy the process of exploring the different types. If you're still not sure it's okay, you may want some extra typing support. There are several great Enneagram experts, like myself, who offer consulting sessions to help you narrow in on your type. I also recommend the book, "The Art of Typing" by Ginger Lapid-Bodga, Ph.D.

Because the Enneagram is very much focused on emotional patterns and behaviors, the assessment itself does occasionally get it wrong. I recommend viewing your results as a starting point. The technology can't see through the influences in your life that might be affecting your answers. Influences like culture, gender, subtype behaviors, stress levels, etc.

Mistyping via assessment is actually more common than you may think. Mistypes can occur because some types have similar behavioral patterns, but the motivation behind those patterns is different (see motivators and fears mentioned a few pages ago). Also, a subtype (which we will get into next) can resemble another type.

Next, I'm going to show graphics of some common mistypes I've seen when using and studying the Enneagram. Please keep in mind any type can be mistyped - not just these. You can use the graphics over the next several pages to help you sort through the types if you feel like you have been mistyped.

Subtypes

Why is it important to understand your subtype for further development work with the Enneagram?

Subtypes help us better understand our core survival instinct, or how we cope with stress. As mentioned earlier, it can also help in mistyping situations. There are three subtypes for each type. This is one reason why there can be so much difference between people of the same type.

Subtype 1

Self-preservation: Governs our needs for material supplies and security, including food, shelter, warmth and family relations.

Subtype 2

Social: Governs our needs for belonging and membership within a larger group and community.

Subtype 3

One-to-one: Governs our sexuality, intimate relationships and close friendships, and the vitality of the life force within our bodies.

Below is a list of how all the subtypes might show up in each type.

Type 1

Self-Preservation: Structure and organization being the utmost importance in order to avoid anxiety. Having control over as much as possible to ensure everything is done right.

Social: Modeling and correcting behavior. Showing the right way to do things so you can ensure people can become better versions of themselves and do the right thing.

One-to-One: A lot of outward intensity toward people and causes that have importance. Believing it's your responsibility to correct and reform them.

Type 2

Self-Preservation: Always giving up your needs and desires for others' needs and desires so they will come to you when they need to feel safe.

Social: Being outspoken and comfortable in situations where the attention is on you to be able to help others. Constantly needing the attention on you to feel worthy of love.

One-to-One: Working on addressing the needs and wants of people in high positions in order to get what you want. Then when you don't get what you want from giving to that person you have feelings of anger and resentment.

Type 3

Self-preservation: Putting an importance on how you are perceived and having structure in your life. You need to be seen as someone who is capable of doing anything and being hardworking to avoid failure.

Social: Needing to be seen socially as someone who is "in the know" and important due to your proximity to people of importance or prestige.

One-to-One: The need for a perfect appearance within your achievements to be seen as successful by people who you admire or are in your close circle.

Type 4

Self-preservation: Self loathing, sitting in negative energy and non-stop thinking about what is happening badly in your life. You may do things you know will turn out badly, but you do them as an adrenaline hit.

Social: Shaming yourself and being self-deprecating with people in your circle in order to gain attention and acceptance, yet you still feel on the outside.

One-to-One: Always sharing your needs, experiences and feelings to those closest to you in order to gain attention and assert dominance.

Type 5

Self-Preservation: Being cognizant about how much of your space and time are occupied by others in order to guard your personal resources.

Social: Developing relationships with a few close people or groups who share your interests. If these people ever become unaligned with those interests you immediately disengage.

One-to-One: Searching for deep connection with one or two people who you trust in order to form protection around yourself and your inner secrets.

Type 6

Self-preservation: Making sure you have a strong support system no matter where you are in order to feel safe. You use these people to reduce your stress and anxiety and bring comfort.

Social: Being a very strict rule follower, and always reminding people around you of these rules to help you feel safe and secure.

One-to-One: Ignoring your own worries and fears by appearing confident and fearless in action in order to help reduce the worries and fears of those closest to you.

Type 7

Self-Preservation: Curating a close knit group of people you enjoy being around regularly, who consistently provide entertainment, help encourage creative thinking and are supportive of your growth.

Social: Offering activity and fun to others first and delayed gratification for yourself. You do this for recognition, which often gives you more stimulation than what you would have had if you were focusing primarily on your needs.

One-to-One: A need to see everyone and everything around you as good, regardless of flaws, to help you cope. You often find that not everyone is as perfect as you dream them to be.

Type 8

Self-preservation: Being aware of what you need in any situation or place to survive. If you can not find what you need, or someone gets in the way, you are quick to anger.

Social: Using your dominance by seeking power, authority and change to protect those you care about or feel are being thwarted in any way.

One-to-One: Seeming to push against rules in a way to gain attention from those around you to gain power and influence over a situation or group of people to assert your dominance and control.

Type 9

Self-preservation: The need for routine and schedule in order to avoid having to actively think about your needs or wants when it comes to your day. You often find attachment to the familiar and comfortable.

Social: Putting all your effort into a group of people, cause or organization to help make significant change in the world in order to avoid focusing on the needs of yourself. Instead, you make your desires merge into the desires of everyone you help.

One-to-One: Building relationships with one or two people and ignoring your needs while focusing all of your attention on their feelings and needs in order to make you feel like you're making a difference.

Explanation of the Diagram

Understanding the Enneagram Diagram is going to be key in your journey. It's important to not only focus on your core type, but all of your connection points within the diagram.

We each have 1 core type, but have 4 other types with which we connect as well, making 5 all together.

1. **Your core type!** This is the main type from which all of the other connections come. This brings awareness to your core motivating factor, fear and emotional patterns.

2 and 3. **Your wings.** Your wings give you a more robust understanding of your personality type.

4. **Your health connection.** The type with which you connect most when in the flow.

5. **Your stress connection.** The type with which you connect most when stressed or headed toward burnout.

Let's go over those in more detail and then discuss what they are for each type.

Everyone has two wings! I like to think of these as your sidekicks. Your main attributes come from your core type, but you can also pick up attributes from the types on either side. Most commonly people will find they pick up attributes more from one wing than another, which is why you might see people say things like, "I'm an Enneagram 3w2." However, our personalities are complex (remember the Enneagram isn't used to put you in a box!) and other people find they pick up attributes from both wings at different times, or no attributes from their wings at all. I personally believe we are our most integrated selves when we can pick up helpful attributes from both wings. Just as a bird needs two wings to fly, we also need two wings to build sustainable strategies both personally and professionally.

Next, we're going to dive into two of the key facets of your Enneagram type as you begin to use it as a self development tool. These are your line of integration, or health line, and line of disintegration, or stress line.

The Enneagram Symbol has lines (or arrows) connecting the different types to one another. The arrow coming from the number that points to your core type is the type you go to in health and the arrow coming out from your core type points to the type you go to in stress. To see how this works within your type, take a look at the diagrams on the following page.

Your health line is connection point number 4. When this line is engaged, it means that in addition to the everyday behaviors and patterns of your core type, you pick up the positive attributes of that type as well. Becoming aware of the positive attributes of your health type will let you know when you are implementing strategies in your life that are working. It's at that moment you should assess what's around you, and consider the steps or processes that brought you there. Then just like the shampoo bottle says: "rinse and repeat!"

Your stress line is connection point number 5. In opposition, when you are in your stress line, you pick up the more challenging patterns or obstacles of that type. For that reason it's important to understand the obstacles that your stress type faces. When you notice those patterns in your life, it's time to stop and assess what's around you. Take a moment to consider the steps and processes which brought you there. Then, look at the strengths of your core type, health type and wings and use those to help you return to center.

Understanding these two types and their relationship to your core type will be helpful in building a sustainable life both personally and professionally.

The next page shows the placement of wings, health type and stress type for each core type.

The Basics | 35

Enneagram Connection Points

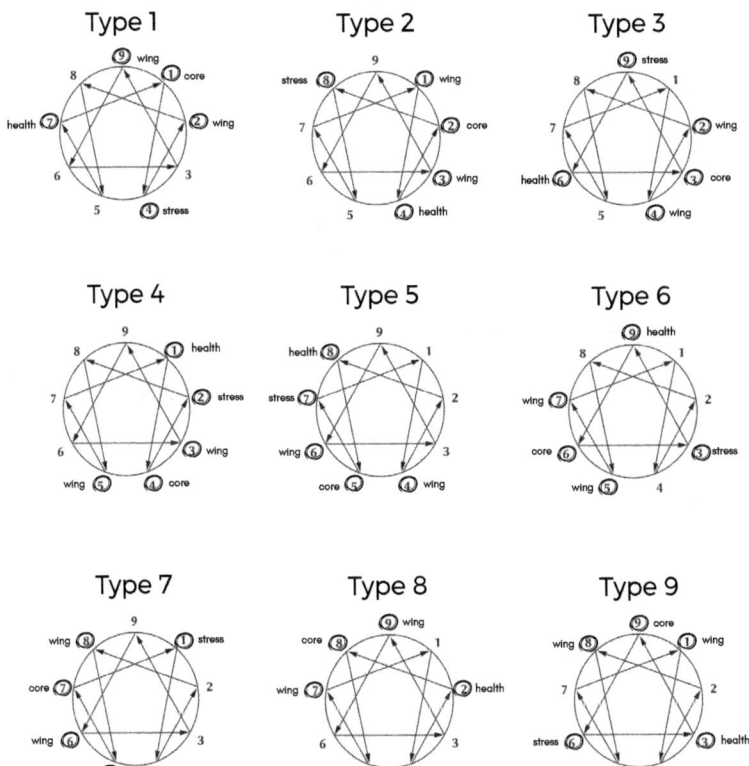

Now that you have a basic understanding of the diagram, below is a general overview of each type and some characteristics each may exhibit professionally.

Type 1: The Perfectionist or The Reformer

Strengths:

- Organized
- Thrive on Routine
- Rule Follower
- Ethical

Common Obstacles:

- Strive for perfection only
- Good is never good enough
- Rigid
- Potential workaholic

Type 2: The Helper or The Giver

Strengths:

- Love to serve
- Responsive
- Well liked
- Relationship builder

Common Obstacles:

- Pour from an empty cup
- Don't take care of yourself
- Get taken advantage of
- Can become resentful

Type 3: The Achiever or The Performer

Strengths:

- Productive
- Create good habits
- Able to prioritize
- Goal oriented

Common Obstacles:

- Quick to burn out
- Care too much what others think
- Overly competitive
- Multitasking

Type 4: The Creative or The Romantic

Strengths:
- Empathetic
- Creative
- Consistent Aesthetic and Branding

Common Obstacles:
- Attachment to a project
- Have to always be in the "mood" to work
- Things can easily get blown out of proportion

Type 5: The Researcher or The Observer

Strengths:
- Research oriented
- Focused
- Expert in field
- Problem solver

Common Obstacles:
- In your head
- Anti-social
- Aloof
- Slow to make decisions

Type 6: The Loyalist or The Skeptic

Strengths:
- Goal setter
- Building contingency plans
- Operations

Common Obstacles:
- Hesitant
- Skeptical
- Fear the worst
- Anxiety peaks with success

Type 7: The Enthusiast or The Serial Entrepreneur

Strengths:

- Multitasking
- Innovative
- Excellent networker

Common Obstacles:

- Ignoring the hard parts of their job
- Not finishing projects
- Invoicing and other mundane business tasks

Type 8: The Challenger or The Boss

Strengths:

- Leader
- Commanding
- Persuasive

Common Obstacles:

- Potential trouble connecting with clients/customers
- All or nothing mentality
- Forceful

Type 9: The Mediator or The Peacemaker

Strengths:

- Passionate
- Respectful
- Dedicated
- Thoughtful

Common Obstacles:

- Making decisions
- Passivity
- Showing your face and skills with confidence

"Our staff has used Enneagram awareness to improve our communication and interaction as we work together. Our staff of approximately 15 full-time and part-time employees makes us more like a large family than a corporation. The Enneagram has given us a helpful and common language to communicate effectively with one another as we work together on projects."

Derek Vreeland, Type 3

Chapter 2

Intelligence Centers

We are constantly forced to make decisions and take action in our personal and professional lives. This can be overwhelming and stressful and is often the reason people become burnt out is that they don't have the proper skills or self awareness to combat this stress.

Decision fatigue is real, am I right?

Believe it or not, this is such a problem that the New York Times Magazine published an article by John Tierney entitled, "Do you suffer from decision fatigue?" about it. I love this excerpt:

"Decision fatigue helps explain why ordinarily sensible people get angry at colleagues and families, splurge on clothes, buy junk food at the supermarket and can't resist the dealer's offer to rustproof their new car. No matter how rational and high-minded you try to be, you can't make decision after decision without paying a biological price. It's different from ordinary physical fatigue — you're not consciously aware of being tired — but you're low on mental energy.

The more choices you make throughout the day, the harder each one becomes for your brain, and eventually it looks for shortcuts."

Understanding how you best make decisions can help you achieve better flow in the decision making process. It's this understanding most people don't realize can be discovered through the Enneagram. The Enneagram is broken down into three intelligence centers. These centers provide the information which helps us best make decisions and take action.

So what are these centers? They are: Head (logic), Heart (feeling) and Body (intuition). I'm going to go over these generally at first, and then dive into each individual type.

The Head Center (types 5, 6 and 7)

These types do best when they take action or make decisions by observing the world. They excel when relying on logic and reasoning to help them work toward a solution. Positive ways to use the head center are to gather information, generate ideas, engage in mental processing, utilize rational analysis and planning.

The Heart Center (types 2, 3 and 4)

These types do best when they take action or make decisions with their feelings or emotions. They excel when relying on their emotions, memories, images and dreams to help them work toward a solution. Positive use of the heart center is to experience feelings, relate to others emotionally and be sensitive to the feelings and reactions of others.

The Body Center* (types 8, 9 and 1)

*also referred to as the gut

These types do best when they rely heavily on instinct and intuition. They excel when they allow themselves space to become present in a situation and reduce potential anger as they work toward a solution. The body center is best used when the person can move around to think, experience physical sensations and is in control of their environment.

In addition to the general advice for each intelligence center, here are some key points for each type to implement for decision making optimization. We will go through each type and discuss some of those points in the form of simple do's and don'ts.

Type 1

When you are making a decision or taking action you unconsciously compare things against your standards of perfection.

- Do give yourself a deadline when decisions need to be made
- Don't pro and con a situation to death
- Do understand that there are some exceptions to the rule
- Don't ignore others' opinions, they will help you expand your view

If you make decisions and take action that way, the critical voice inside of you will dissolve and positive action can be taken.

Type 2

When making a decision, you constantly keep a running list of the likes, dislikes, hopes and dreams of others.

- Don't think only about the implications on others, think also about the implications it has on you
- Do let your feelings and emotions guide you toward the solution or next step
- Don't forget to bring facts to support your feelings
- Do be empathic, but beware of personally emotionally manipulating a situation

If you make decisions and take action with those things in mind, your real needs can surface and you can discover your own path, instead of backing up and helping with everyone else's.

Type 3

When making a decision you are always in convergent thinking, meaning any idea that has ever worked for you in another place is now aimed at your current goal.

- Don't be rash and make a decision in the moment based strictly on emotion
- Do use your heart to authentically relate to a situation, but be cautious of role playing
- Don't make a decision based solely on what you think others will think
- Do use your gift for taking action and making decisions in a timely fashion

If you make decisions and take action with these things in mind, your personal feelings will be allowed to arise. You will take the time to think about important questions about what could cause issues in the future - not only in the present. You'll be in position to discover the right decision instead of taking the quickest action.

Type 4

When making a decision or taking action you unconsciously exaggerate what you can't have, then by comparison, what you do actually have seems insignificant.

- Do use your heart for compassion toward a situation or important decision
- Don't become overly sensitive toward an issue
- Do connect with the problem on a deep level
- Don't over dramatize the situation

If you keep these things in mind when making a decision or taking action, you will find the next step is clear, precise and without emotional baggage.

Type 5

When you are making a decision or taking action you will find yourself stretching your cognitive ability.

- Do use your head to objectively analyze
- Don't over analyze
- Do research the situation
- Don't rely on solely your own experiences and resources, consult others

If you do these things when making a decision or taking action you will be able to be direct and confident in your decision, while not withholding your opinion.

Type 6

When making a decision or taking action, you will find yourself often saying what if? Is this true? What about the other side of the problem?

- Do use your head to bring insight to possible problems or errors
- Don't project problems that aren't there
- Do find peace in knowing you've thought of everything
- Don't continue to create scenarios after your decision is already made

If you do these things when making decisions or taking action you will be able to accept with confidence that the right decision has been made and the outcome will be positive.

Type 7

When making decisions or taking action you combine a number of positive ways to execute a plan or come to a conclusion.

- Do use your head to productively plan ahead
- Don't overplan yourself into perfectionism
- Do allow yourself to think of all the best possible situations
- Don't shy away from something just because it's uncomfortable

If you do these things when making a decision or taking action you will be able to find peace in your decision and be undistracted by outside stimuli.

Type 8

When you are making a decision or taking action you have an all or nothing mentality.

- Do use your instincts to take action or make a decision
- Don't be forceful in your actions or decisions
- Do allow yourself to release anger by performing a stress relieving activity first
- Don't let anger control your decisions and actions

If you're able to do these things when making a decision, or taking action, you will feel more empowered. You will also find that you take both yourself and others into consideration when determining the best overall outcome.

Type 9

When making decisions or taking action you naturally process all the angles of that decision and forget about your needs.

- Do use your instincts to mediate or work through a problem
- Don't become passive and avoid the problem
- Do allow yourself to feel worry or angst in your body when making a decision or taking action
- Don't make a decision out of only wanting the conflict or decision making process to be over

If you do these things when making a decision or taking action you will avoid procrastinating and make a decision that works best for you.

Personally, uncovering my center of intelligence has been one of the biggest components of my success. Once I understood that my feelings and emotions as a type 3 were positive, I felt authentically myself when making decisions or taking action in my business. No one knows you better than yourself, so trust in your ability to make a decision or take actions with these steps!

"Before I was a full time photographer, I was an elementary and high school teacher for 4 years. By working in a school setting, surrounded by people constantly (students and coworkers/bosses), I've learned a lot about myself and how I operate between relationships and work. Now that I am full time with photography, my day to day life looks completely different. I am personally super grateful for the Enneagram because it's helped me put language to how I'm feeling and acting in different situations especially with all the change that has happened in my life recently."

Morgan, Type 7

Chapter 3
Communication

Communication is fundamental to our existence; whether personally between peers and family, or professionally with clients or co-workers.

Communication can make or break relationships, set the tone in an environment, propel us forward or hold us back. Communication development is not only about learning how you communicate, but how to do so with others most effectively.

With regard to communication, it's important not only to pay attention to your type, but to all nine types. Understanding your type will allow you to recognize your communication patterns and express your needs to others, but understanding the other types allows you to hold more space, grace and empathy for them and their patterns. Which is where real self-development is found.

So here we go. We are going to discuss verbal and non-verbal cues each type gives as well as positive and challenging habits of each type.

Also, a friendly reminder, just because this is your innate communication style, it doesn't give you a pass in the challenges department. Through awareness of the challenges you can focus on how to overcome them.

Type 1

Verbal Cues: Use of words like ought, should, right, wrong, must. Verbal communication is direct and detailed.

Non-verbal cues: Tight jaw, focus on posture, self-control.

As a type 1 you have the following habits: Accept responsibility, practical, detailed and inspiring.

Some challenges you may face are: Being critical, defensive and forceful.

Type 2

Verbal Cues: Asking a lot of questions, complimentary and soft in tone. Communication is nice and feeling centered.

Non-verbal cues: Smile, eye contact and engaged shoulders.

As a Type 2 you have the following habits: You make people feel special. You are caring, easy to talk to, are sensitive to needs, energetic and expressive.

Some challenges you may face are: Being demanding when it comes to your need for information and connection, manipulative and disengaged if you don't like the person.

Type 3

Verbal cues: Gets to the point quickly, concise, speaks in three point format.

Non-verbal cues: Engaged eyes, a lot of energy and confident demeanor.

As a type 3 you have the following habits: You are energetic, a constant encourager, optimistic and practical.

Some challenges you may face are: You can come off as fake or superficial because you have the ability to change your tone to match whoever you're around, you can often soften the truth and appear manipulative.

Type 4

Verbal cues: Long and feeling based conversations. Frequent use of me, my, I to bring connectivity. Enjoy deep topics and conversation.

Non-verbal cues: Intense, touchy, wear emotions on their face

As a type 4 you have the following habits: You enjoy listening and talking for long periods of time. You don't mind sharing personal experiences.

Some challenges you may face are: Due to sharing so many of your own experiences you can make people feel like they're not enough or their experience doesn't match up. You can also make people think your feelings/emotions are more important than theirs.

Type 5

Verbal cues: Don't actually speak a lot. When they do speak they use succinct language or talk at length if it's a topic they know about. It's feast or famine with words.

Non-verbal cues: Minimal eye-contact, detached, very little facial expression.

As a type 5 you have the following habits: Taking in information before you engage. Calm disposition, especially in crisis.

Some challenges you may face are: You focus more on facts than feelings. Can make people feel unwanted and can send signals of superiority and arrogance.

Type 6

Verbal cues: Ask a lot of what if questions, use of words that are quantifiable like measurements, quantities, etc. Are actively solving problems.

Non-verbal cues: Active eyes, bouncing knees or moving arms, can appear always stressed/anxious.

As a type 6 you have the following habits: Asking a lot of questions and need for information. Make people feel appreciated for who they are.

Some challenges you may face are: You can come off as intense and can make people feel like they don't have it together because you are always questioning.

Type 7

Verbal Cues: Talk fast, conversation can seem all over the place, engaging and tell a lot of stories. Reframe negative situations.

Non-verbal cues: A lot of facial expressions and can appear distracted.

As a type 7 you can have the following habits: Adding to the conversation before a point is finalized, frequent making of jokes, adding creative perspective and always talking about and seeing the best in every situation.

Some challenges you may face are: Checking out of confrontational conversation, dismissing feelings and giving off tones of superiority to people who you don't like.

Type 8

Verbal Cues: Strong language, big words, commanding sentence structure.

Non-verbal cues: Strong appearance, hands on hips, assertive, resting ----- face.

As a type 8 you can have the following habits: You are always right to the point, you use an impactful tone and can empower people with your words.

Some challenges you may face are: You can be perceived as abrasive and make people feel dumb if they don't agree with you. You can switch your communication style to anger with little provocation.

Type 9

Verbal Cues: Are very agreeable and use language like, I see, oh interesting, mhmm. They speak in sequence and give a lot of background information on their thought process.

Non-verbal cues: Relaxed, welcoming eyes, posture for listening and receiving.

As a type 9 you have the following habits: You listen (and think) before you speak, you are diplomatic, you enjoy shooting the breeze with people to develop rapport.

Some challenges you may face are: You tend to space out during stress. You can be passive aggressive and don't always express your frustrations.

"Emotional intelligence is a journey, really like a continuous journey all throughout our lives. It really increases with conscious effort. We grow in our emotional intelligence, despite aging, up to a certain point, but identifying my Enneagram type, has been life-changing because it created more self-awareness for me, which is the foundation of emotional intelligence. We have to be self-aware to grow in our social awareness, in all of our relationships and how to manage our emotions in an effective and healthy way. Working to identify my Enneagram type brought peace to me of like, okay, this is who I really am."

Katie, Type 9

Chapter 4

Fighting Burnout

In Chapter 1, I mentioned that understanding your line of stress on the Enneagram diagram can help to avoid burnout.

But what is burnout?

According to an article by HelpGuide.org, burnout is "a state of emotional, physical, and mental exhaustion caused by excessive and prolonged stress. It occurs when you feel overwhelmed, emotionally drained, and unable to meet constant demands."

Burnout is something we all experience at one point or another. Whether you're a business owner, head of a company or a key team member. Burnout is real and can happen more often than not if we don't become carefully aware of the emotions and actions that lead us there.

Don't take my word for it, look at these stats:

According to the Harvard Business Review in their article entitled, "What Makes Entrepreneurs Burn Out?" by Eva de Mol,

Jeff Pollack, and Violet T. Ho "Entrepreneurs are more at risk of burnout because they tend to be extremely passionate about work and more socially isolated, have limited safety nets, and operate in high uncertainty."

In the article, they quoted a study from 2017 that said, "78% of startup owners (businesses less than two years old) report burnout. That percentage increases as the business ages. Businesses from years 2 to 10 experience the highest burnout, at 86%."

Additionally, an article published by Vantage Circle quoted a study from Gallup, an American analytics and advisory company based in Washington, D.C., that said "out of 7,500 employees [surveyed] 23% reported burnout. 63% of employees are more likely to call in for sick day leaves if they are facing burnout at work or are facing personal issues. And even if they do not call in for leaves, their performance is likely to reduce by 13%."

Do these statistics shock you? At first, they shocked me too. But after years of working with business owners and teams it became clear to me that we just aren't taught how to avoid burnout.

What causes burnout and can we prevent it? What is the path that leads to this state of emotional, physical and mental exhaustion and can we learn to interrupt that path? Yes!

I believe the reason for this burnout epidemic is that we don't know how to best operate for our unique personalities nor to recognize the signs our bodies give us to slow down and interrupt the path.

So let's take a look at how the Enneagram can help you stop burnout before it happens, or reduce it and turn the tables back to a path of growth.

The key factor in burnout is stress, both professionally and personally. Here is a breakdown of where each type goes to in stress.

> Type 1 -> Type 4
>
> Type 2 -> Type 8
>
> Type 3 -> Type 9
>
> Type 4 -> Type 2
>
> Type 5 -> Type 7
>
> Type 6 -> Type 3
>
> Type 7 -> Type 1
>
> Type 8 -> Type 5
>
> Type 9 -> Type 6

An important thing to remember about stress lines is that when you go to your stress type, you tend to only pick up the more challenging attributes of that type. Additionally, since your internal operating system isn't wired to deal with those attributes on a regular basis, you will find them exaggerated. For example, a type 1 is used to battling perfection and the stress that it can cause in their life. Their body is naturally able to better cope with those feelings. In opposition, a type 7 who goes to a type 1 in stress, does not have the innate ability to cope with the emotion that perfection can bring, making burnout more likely.

The following are a few signs and emotional cues to help each type recognize when they're heading toward burnout.

Type 1: You are easily angered at minor inconveniences and feel as though no one understands what you're going through.

Emotional Cues: moody, drained, more emotional than usual

Type 2: You begin to feel controlled by your life or job, and can't remember the last time you did something for yourself without anyone else benefitting.

Emotional Cues: demanding, aggressive, unapproachable

Type 3: You start "numbing" to avoid the feeling of not being good enough. Things like zoning out on your phone, mindlessly binge watching television, etc.

Emotional Cues: melancholy, ambivalent, ignorance is bliss

Type 4: You start hyper-focusing on the problems of those around you to help you feel a sense of purpose from others needing you.

Emotional Cues: resentment, self-pity, neglecting yourself

Type 5: You become easily distracted and are unable to focus.

Emotional Cues: scattered thinking, directionless, critical

Type 6: You become too focused on a project and neglect everything else in your life.

Emotional Cues: high energy followed by a crash, self-critical, workaholic

Type 7: You begin experiencing feelings of perfectionism or believe there is only one "right" way to do things.

Emotional Cues: rigid, anger, perfectionism

Type 8: You withdraw from others and neglect your own well-being.

Emotional Cues: in your head, anti-social, quiet

Type 9: You experience increased worry and become more reactive than thoughtful

Emotional Cues: anxious, scattered, hesitant

Once you notice these behaviors, you can then employ these tips to help you head back to integration.

Type 1: Focus on happy emotions and participate in spontaneous activity. This could mean stepping away from work (completely) for a day to do something that brings you joy.

Type 2: Turn your focus inward to the needs of yourself just as much as the needs of others. When you are healthy, self-care should be a top priority.

Type 3: Think about all sides of the situation and lean into the operations and strategy behind it. See the task or project all the way through, even if you think it will fail. Don't "abort the mission"- trust yourself and the plan you created.

Type 4: Take time to step back in order to be more objective. Separate your feelings from the situation and focus on the task at hand. For example: write out a "feeling dump" in a journal before heading back to your task.

Type 5: If possible, step into a more leadership focused role and take on more challenges. You might find yourself coming out of your shell more when in an integrated state.

Type 6: Use deep breathing and mindfulness to embrace going with the flow. Recognize and name all of the things that are going well in your life or business.

Type 7: Focus on redirecting your desire from multitasking to finishing a single project. Key into the projects you are truly passionate about rather than the next shiny object.

Type 8: Put emphasis on being comfortable with your feelings and embracing a spirit of giving. You can embody this by focusing more on helping others than being "right."

Type 9: Take hold of your confidence. Instead of worrying what people think and how you might be understood by them. Be present in the moment and speak your truth. When you are healthy you will be ready to tackle new goals with fresh perspective and zeal.

As you use the Enneagram more in your self-development journey, these strategies to keep stress at a distance will become easier. Change won't happen overnight, but this awareness will soon help you take important action to unlock your potential at work. We will learn more about turning this awareness into action in Chapter 7.

"I have a greater understanding of my fellow team members and a sense of bonding over the use of the enneagram as a common language to understand ourselves better."

Chelsea Bell, Type 6

Chapter 5
Time Management

There is no "one size fits all" strategy for time management, and for good reason. Our brains are uniquely wired when it comes to time and what works for one person may not work for someone else. Think about which of these works best for you:

- Weekly/monthly planning ahead
- Time blocking
- Daily priorities vs. to-do Lists
- Time auditing
- Doing most important tasks first

The list of different strategies can go on and the one you prefer may not have even been included. Time means something different to everybody. I've put together a funny look at how each type relates to time, so have a laugh before we dig in!

When you hear the word time....

Type 1: There is a right way to use it.

Type 2: I want to give mine all away.

Type 3: Never enough.

Type 4: Is precious and valuable.

Type 5: What about it?

Type 6: I want to make the best use of it.

Type 7: Always enough!

Type 8: Is mine to use.

Type 9: Is a construct.

While the list above was compiled for fun, it's likely you found it true for your type.

It's important to find time management strategies that work best for you based on your unique personality. I am sharing the following basic tips and tools to help you find success in this area. These techniques are just the starting point, pay attention to what works for you and implement them for continued growth.

Type 1

Unintentional procrastination is a common time management problem for this type. It arises from their need to be sure everything is done the "right" way. They will double, even triple check, their work which leads to missed deadlines and burnout. The fear of making a mistake can prevent them from putting out any final work at all.

If you're a type 1, doing the following may help to increase your time management skills:

- Learn to trust others and delegate tasks. You can't be an expert at everything! Audit your time and identify tasks that are taking you the most time and find a way to outsource or delegate. What takes you five hours could take an expert in that task two. You will have more time to focus on the things you're good at and keep your project moving.
- Break your project into smaller daily tasks instead of trying to do it all at once. You will feel more productive if you can check items off your list. This method will also allow you to step away from the project when your scheduled parts of the project for the day are done.

Type 2

Filling their day with too much is a common time management problem for this type. This type feels compelled to answer a need immediately. They fill every day with as many tasks as possible to help others or improve their workplace. They have a hard time prioritizing tasks and discerning immediate needs from nonimmediate.

If you're a type 2, doing the following can help to increase your time management skills:

- Remain focused on the tasks of the day, and avoid picking up additional tasks from others before completing your own.
- Block periods of time alone to complete tasks and avoid interruptions. This means turning all notifications off as well!

Type 3

A common time management problem for type 3 is acting before planning. When they get an idea (especially if it relates to increased profits) they run with it before dedicating time to evaluate pros and cons or develop a solid strategy. This often leads to a project that doesn't perform as well as hoped.

If you're a type 3, the following can help increase your time management skills:

- Slow down while working to avoid mistakes and having to re-do a task or project. Take the time to build a strategy before hitting the ground running.
- Create daily priorities from your to-do list to avoid powering through everything at once. This will help you feel more productive and avoid burnout.

Type 4

The urge to find purpose and feeling in each moment is a common time management problem for type 4. It distracts them from time sensitive tasks. They often don't recognize time when in the creative space, regularly realizing that what they thought might take them an hour takes four. Thus they don't like to put time frames on anything to feel more at ease with the process.

If you're a type 4, you can do the following to help increase your time management skills:

- Group monotonous tasks and time block them into your week to prevent avoidance of tasks that don't excite you. Create a comfortable and consistent environment to do these tasks to train your brain to recognize it's time to work. Engage all the five senses for optimal training of the brain.
- Do the most important tasks of your day first and allow your creative tasks to be your reward. It may also help to set a timer for your creative tasks to ensure the other priorities of the day are also completed.

Type 5

Mismanaging energy is a common time management problem for this type. Most people of this type thrive on alone time to recharge. If they over schedule themselves without space to be alone, they may not be able to properly focus on tasks. This will leave them feeling scattered and as though nothing was accomplished.

If you're a type 5, the following may help to increase your time management skills:

- Create a dedicated space for work which is free of distractions. Let others know this is your work space and to avoid interrupting.

- Set a project timeline to avoid working on one task for too long. This will help decrease scattered feelings in times of stress, and will also keep you on track. It is especially important to adhere to the timeline to avoid stalling in the research and preparing phase.

Type 6

Over planning and preparing is a common time management problem for the type 6. The fear of "what if" scenarios prevents them from moving forward efficiently. This type will ensure they are making the best use of each moment and that all bases are covered. This happens most often when the project or task is for themselves rather than a client or work related task.

If you're a type 6, doing the following can increase your time management skills:

- Avoid starting and stopping a task. By seeing a task through to completion, you are less likely to backtrack to review your work multiple times. This helps prevent unintentional procrastination.
- Prioritize tasks for yourself in the same way you prioritize tasks for others. Implement the same systems you've created for others for yourself.

Type 7

A common time management problem for this type is the misconception that they have more time than they actually do. Due to this type's need for doing a variety of tasks and having a variety of interests, time is restrictive and unimportant to them. They don't do well with a lot of structure and consistently avoid tasks they consider boring or joyless. These patterns often delay projects and deadlines become elusive.

If you're type 7, you can start by doing the following to increase your time management skills:

- Set aside a block of time each day for new projects rather than interrupting a task to brainstorm or work on something new.
- Build in rewards after completed tasks to avoid unfinished projects. This can be something like working on a passion project after the 'boring' tasks are finished.

Type 8

A common time management problem for this type is allowing the need for control to trump everything. This type often takes on too many tasks which forces them to power through projects without time to check for errors before completion, but they still expect the project to be great and get angry if it isn't.

If you're a type 8, the following may help increase your time management skills:

- Find the value in building a team instead of pushing through alone. It will help you increase productivity and avoid burnout.
- Schedule in time for weekly evaluations of your work. This will allow you to assess if a pivot needs to be made, and time to make it, before a project is completed.

Type 9

A common time management problem for this type is following the day rather than leading it. They also spend a lot of time weighing options and delaying action until the last minute, if at all. They put emphasis on the amount of thought put into everything they do, so without clear guidelines and structure nothing is completed.

If you're a type 9, doing the following may help increase your time management skills:

- Create structure in your work by either time blocking or having recurring check-ins with either someone on your team or an accountability partner.
- Set clear deadlines for projects with accountability to avoid procrastination and time spent on endless pro and con lists.

Regardless of type, taking regular breaks should be a part of your time management strategy. Resting allows your mind and body to reset which is good for productivity as well as overall comfort in your work day (think tired eyes from looking at a computer, or tight hips from sitting in one place!).

Once you become familiar with the patterns and tips for your type, I encourage you to begin exploring the other types. Understanding how alternative types manage time will help you build stronger relationships and teams.

"Being aware of my struggles has helped me put systems into place that keep me on track better than before I applied the Enneagram (like time-blocking or working on one project at a time to completion before moving on). I am also more aware of when I need to take breaks and allow myself to rest before diving back in so I am not working out of resentment."

Brittany, Type 8

Chapter 6
Leadership

I wanted to start this chapter with a definition of leadership. As I was searching for the perfect definition, it was immediately obvious that they were all very vague, without any clear definition.

I started broad using Google's dictionary:

Leadership- the action of leading a group of people or an organization.

Leader- the person who leads or commands a group, organization or country.

Lead- to guide in a way often by going ahead; to be at the head or front part; to be best, first or ahead.

Then I dug further, looking for the qualities of good leadership rather than a specific definition.

A Gallup article entitled, *"Why Great Managers are so Rare,"* by Randall J. Beck and Jim Harter indicated some of these traits:

- Assertiveness
- Motivation
- Creates accountability
- Ability to build relationships
- Ability to make decisions based on productivity not politics

The Center for Creative Leadership in their article, "The Characteristics & Qualities of a Good Leader" indicated these qualities:

- Integrity
- Ability to delegate
- Communication
- Self-Awareness
- Gratitude
- Learning agility
- Influence
- Empathy
- Courage
- Respect

I could quote several other groups as well, all with similarities and differences. Leadership looks different everywhere. In some countries, it looks quiet, calm and direct. In others it looks assertive, bold and controlling.

However, I'm a firm believer that no matter if you're in business for yourself, or part of an organization or team, everyone has the ability to be a leader and harness their unique personality to become a better one. I do believe the ability to lead is innate, meaning leading can definitely be harder for some than others.

Although each type has a plethora of strengths and common obstacles, to remain true to the quick self-development tips in this book, I will list the top three strengths and common obstacles. In addition, I am including three tips on how to work with or for each leader.

There are so many nuances in leadership dependent on sexuality, culture, industry, and many other factors. This is obvious given that no one can agree on a definition.

It is my hope that someday this will change. I hope we will learn to be aware of ourselves and others in a way that is empathetic as we focus on healthy self-development. After all, that is why I am writing this book!

I would like to note, it is also important to note that common obstacles are just that, obstacles- not roadblocks. With awareness of these obstacles, comes the ability to use your strengths to overcome them, allowing yourself to take hold of your most badass leadership qualities.

Let's get to it.

Type 1

Strengths:
- Practice what they preach
- Quality is of the utmost importance
- Organized

Common Obstacles:
- Controlling
- Defensive
- Critical

Working with this type of leader:
- Be able to handle being micromanaged
- Be extremely detail oriented
- Be able to own your mistakes

Type 2

Strengths:
- Relationship builder
- Great motivator
- Empathetic to needs of those around them

Common Obstacles:
- Boundaries with time
- Can be passive aggressive
- Can easily become resentful of work if they overextend

Working with this type of leader:
- Be generous with compliments
- Be cognizant of appearance and how you represent the company
- Be a team player

Type 3

Strengths:
- Results driven
- Reads a room well
- Confident and optimistic

Obstacles:
- Overextends easily
- Impatient
- Creates a competitive environment

Working with this type of leader:
- Be self-motivated
- Be willing to work overtime
- Bring ideas to the table

Type 4

Strengths:
- Creativity
- Relationship building
- Expressive and inspiring

Common Obstacles:
- Moody
- Have a hard time receiving negative feedback
- Can be deeply critical of others

Working with this type of leader:
- Do not be sensitive to criticism
- High attention to detail when it comes to presentation
- The ability to be vulnerable

Type 5

Strengths:

- Objective
- Analytical
- Persistent

Common Obstacles:

- Seeming aloof
- Stubborn
- Can be hyper critical of others

Working with this type of leader:

- Always come overly prepared for meetings
- Be okay with working alone
- Have thick skin

Type 6

Strengths:

- Turning around a bad situation or troubleshooting
- Organization
- Loyalty to employees and team

Common Obstacles:

- Delays in decision making
- Fear peaks at success
- Enhanced focus on flaws

Working with this type of leader:

- Don't hesitate to give constructive feedback on a project
- Cover your bases, don't let them find holes in your project
- Be as soft spoken as possible to not threaten their leadership

Type 7

Strengths:

- Team building
- Can synthesize data and make decisions quickly
- Innovative

Common Obstacles:

- Don't take negative feedback well
- Can lack focus
- Dislike routine

Working with this type of leader:

- Be prepared for schedule changes
- Have good follow through
- Don't shoot ideas down immediately

Type 8

Strengths:

- Direct or assertive
- Directing strategy and deployment
- Protective of their people

Common Obstacles:

- Misplaced anger
- Daily management of team
- Major on the minors

Working with this type of leader:

- Don't soften or manipulate information, be as direct as possible
- Don't expect a lot of compliments or praise
- Keep them abreast of any new information as much as possible

Type 9

Strengths:

- Creating vision
- Collecting information
- Ensures everyone in the organization or team feels heard (mediator)

Common Obstacles:

- Slow to make decisions
- Giving clear direction
- Evasive during direct conflict

Working with this type of leader:

- Be self-motivated
- Pay attention to detail to help accomplish vision
- Avoid putting pressure on tasks or goals

As a reminder, the Enneagram is not an excuse for bad behavior. Awareness of these common obstacles is meant to encourage us to be mindful of our actions. Use this insight to do the tough self-development work, push through those obstacles and overcome them.

Use this reference list for a quick snapshot at how each leader type may manage:

Type 1: Leads by example.

Type 2: Develops rapport by building relationships.

Type 3: Pushes for productivity.

Type 4: Inventive and poignant in actions.

Type 5: Works from outside looking in.

Type 6: Micromanage.

Type 7: Casual and innovative.

Type 8: Dominant presence.

Type 9: Relaxed and thoughtful.

"My biggest take away with the Enneagram as a program coordinator is a deeper understanding of my team. Learning from them in the best ways to communicate with them, areas of strengths, and areas of growth. I am able individualize my approach with each staff member meeting their needs in a way that they will respond to. In my own self growth I learned I am able to reflect and realize my actions and what could be causing them, and when to take some self- care actions to get me into a better place. I still have a lot to learn about applications of the Enneagram but I feel like I have become a better guide and coach for my team, and on the flip side being open with my team has allowed them to see the big picture from my program and better understand my personality and what runs through my head on the daily."

- Tyler Kearns, Type 6

Chapter 7
Overcoming Obstacles

I have yet to meet someone without obstacles in their life. One of the things I love about the Enneagram is how it brings empathy both for others and ourselves around potential obstacles. The list below is composed of common obstacles for each Enneagram type at work. I list these things not to provide an excuse, but to show you that you're not alone.

It is important to remember that everyone is different and as a result, will have different struggles. Self-development level, cultural overlays, gender overlays, and other factors, in addition to core type contribute to these obstacles.

This is just a glance inside what obstacles each type *might* experience professionally.

Type 1

- Perfectionism
- Delegation
- Pressure around time
- Expressing emotion
- Critical Eye
- Workaholic

Type 2

- Resentment of work
- Always feel behind
- Organization
- Setting priorities
- Feel unappreciated
- Not feeling heard

Type 3

- Workaholic
- Consistency
- People pleaser
- Never ending to-dos
- Fear of missing out
- Imposter syndrome

Type 4

- Sensitive to criticism
- Moodiness
- Time management
- Feeling misunderstood
- Scatterbrained
- Overextended

Type 5

- Overwhelmed/drained
- Accepting feedback
- Communication
- Lack of direction
- Confidence
- Boundaries

Type 6

- Analysis paralysis
- Fear of success
- Procrastination
- Burnout
- Feel unappreciated
- Doubt in abilities

Type 7

- Organization
- Routine/structure
- Appearing engaged in meetings
- Time management
- Unfinished projects
- Receiving negative feedback

Type 8

- Details
- Working in a team
- Pivoting quickly
- Time management
- Misplaced anger
- Appearing controlling

Type 9

- Time management
- Not being assertive
- Decision making
- Lack of structure
- Overwhelm
- Get taken advantage of

Overcoming Obstacles | 91

In previous chapters, you've learned about your wings, health and stress lines, center of intelligence and more. You are developing an awareness of these for your type, but applying that knowledge is where real self-development takes place. Application is how you use the Enneagram to help overcome obstacles at work - or at home for that matter!

I strongly believe we have all the tools we need to overcome the obstacles we face in our day to day life. *You* are the key to your success and have everything you need is right inside you. What may be missing is learning how to unlock it. I'm about to show you how.

When an obstacle arises, here are some questions to ask yourself to helm overcome and grow through it:

- What strengths can my health line bring to the table?
- How can my intelligence center help me?
- What strengths from my wings will compliment my core type's strengths and offset the challenging traits?

Below are just suggested answers to these questions. If you need to, return to Chapter 1 and review the work you did highlighting the characteristics from each of the connection points you resonate with most, do that now.

Type 1

Engage 9 wing: Relax and reflect

Engage 2 wing: Focus on who or what things impact first, then the task or project at hand

Engage 7 health line: Explore possibilities, ask what if questions

Type 2

Engage 1 wing: Bring in objectivity and discernment

Engage 3 wing: Seek respect from yourself, not just from others

Engage 4 health line: Address your feelings, validate them and take action

Type 3

Engage 2 wing: Show more empathy to yourself and others

Engage 4 wing: Think creatively

Engage 6 health line: Push yourself for factual honesty around the situation

Type 4

Engage 3 wing: Stay in control of your feelings

Engage 5 wing: Value your logical mind

Engage 1 health line: Become objective and take action

Type 5

Engage 4 wing: Make connections with others

Engage 6 wing: Think of ways your knowledge can benefit those around you

Engage 8 health line: Take your seat at the table

Type 6

Engage 5 wing: Work on containment of thoughts

Engage 7 wing: Relax and have fun

Engage 9 health line: Experiment with going with the flow

Type 7

Engage 6 wing: Face all sides of a situation, even the negative

Engage 8 wing: Be clear and direct in your words and activities

Engage 5 health line: Spend time alone in the quiet

Type 8

Engage 7 wing: Lighten up your outlook

Engage 9 wing: Listen as much as you talk

Engage 2 health line: Look for ways to increase empathy

Type 9

Engage 8 wing: Understand your own needs

Engage 1 wing: Build structure

Engage 3 health line: Develop key result metrics

Example Exercises to Help Overcome Obstacles

Type 1

To help overcome obstacles, start by asking yourself questions that are thought provoking (engaging your primary center of the body) and exploratory (engaging your health line's center of the head)questions. For example:

Why would I want to let go of that anger/hurt? Why wouldn't I want to let go of that anger/hurt?

Close your eyes and experience the feelings of both sides of the question. How does it make you feel from your head, down to your toes. This will help engage your body in the action and bring you to a more grounded place.

What if I delegated a task? What if I didn't?

Let your mind bring you new thoughts and facts. How can you bring logic and reasoning around the obstacles you face? This will help you to be more objective and bring less emotion to the obstacle.

Type 2

Your primary and health line centers are the heart. To help overcome obstacles, it will be key to engage feelings both externally and internally.

To help engage these feelings, try journaling. Instead of only asking how does this affect others, also ask how does this affect me? Bring both the internal and external feelings together. Ensure you regularly check-in with yourself as much as you with those around you. Incorporating this sort of journal check-in allows you to work through obstacles instead of avoiding them, and may reduce the amount you encounter and your resentment level.

Type 3

Access your primary center of the heart and your health line's center of the head. To help overcome obstacles, I recommend first writing out all your feelings around the issue at hand. This will provide a way for you to recognize and validate them. Write out facts to help you prove or disprove the feelings. You will often find when doing this exercise that you can look more objectively at your obstacles.

It's important to note that if you disprove the feeling, it doesn't mean failure. It means you're working through it.

Type 4

To help overcome obstacles, engage in a body scan to access your health line's intelligence center of body. Go to a quiet place and imagine experiencing the obstacle. Then scan how every part of your body feels while experiencing that obstacle.

Follow the initial body scan with a feeling dump. In a journal, write everything you felt, validate the feelings and get them out of your system. Use this to open more space for positive feelings around overcoming the obstacle. Now imagine not having to experience the obstacle, then scan your body again. Finally, write down the next best actionable step you can take to get you to an unobstructed place.

Type 5

To assist in overcoming obstacles, access your primary center of the head by spending time thinking about who you can bring in to help you find the answers outside your own knowledge. Implement the proverb that two heads are better than one. While honoring your opinion, adding someone else's thoughts could help you to overcome the obstacle.

While working through the obstacle, ensure your opinion is heard. To access your health line's center of body, notice how your body feels when you do and don't speak up. Bring to mind those thoughts when you need an extra push.

Type 6

As you work through overcoming obstacles, work on trusting yourself as much as others trust you. Access your primary center of the head by guiding yourself through a thought process that considers the best case scenario instead of only the worst.

Access your health line's center of the body by creating time to time to physically relax. Create a list of activities you find relaxing. When you catch yourself overthinking an obstacle, return to that list of tried and true activities. Select one stress relieving activity to do before you spend any more time on the obstacle. You may find that you come back with a clearer mind.

Type 7

Your primary center and health line centers are the head. To overcome obstacles, it will be important to slow your thoughts and narrow your focus. Instead of thinking (or not thinking) about everything contributing to the obstacle, pick one item to focus on. The goal is to not only quiet your thoughts, but also the environment you're in to work through them.

Allow yourself to dig into the obstacle one piece at a time instead of jumping around or worse, ignoring it altogether.

Type 8

Access your primary center of the body when overcoming obstacles and find a quiet place. Use this space to focus on how your body feels and try naming the feeling. The intention is to bring you back to your core center (body) and engage your health line's center of the heart (feeling).

Once you are grounded and centered, begin to explore ways to work through the obstacle. Consider the pros and cons as they would impact yourself and others. The solution should not only bring peace to you, but to those who surround you as well.

Type 9

Like the rest of the body center types, it's extremely important to find a place of center and grounding, whatever that means for you. This could mean doing yoga or meditation, walking outside barefoot or a body scan. The goal is to bring awareness to the feelings in your body and to identify them.

Once in touch with your body, journal about what you want from the situation. Pay particular attention to your needs and your requests while removing focus from what you think others want. This allows you to access your health line's center of the heart while problem solving.

"I have found that with an understanding of the Enneagram, it is easier to navigate my day with a better understanding of effective communication with my peers. I no longer take things personally when I see someone with less than optimal behavior or responses, especially when it's during interaction with me."
Laura, Type 5

Chapter 8
Real Life, Enneagram at Work

If every chapter so far has been adding another level to the building, then consider this the roof! I'm going to bring you real life work challenges from each type drawn from conversations I've h ad with folks of all types in different professions. Some were self-employed, others worked in organizations and some a mixture of both. I'm sharing some excerpts from those conversations in hopes you will see:

1. You're not alone.

2. Enneagram coaching in action as a way to help you overcome common obstacles.

Please Note: Transcripts have been edited to provide better clarity for the reader.

Type 1
Phillipa Channer
Digital Marketing Coach

Phillipa came to me struggling with how much she needed her clients to know, like and trust her immediately, before taking the time necessary for these things to happen organically. Here is an excerpt from our conversation.

"As a type 1 your core motivation in life is to be good or right and to have integrity, but because this is how your internal operating system works, it's easy to assume that's how everyone will immediately see you. But trust is hard to build for some people. So the goal here is how can you (1) strengthen your mindset around the fact that you don't need that immediate trust to be successful and (2) use your strengths to help you gain the trust you crave from your clients?

We will start with number one, strengthening your mindset. Lean into your health type of a 7 and explore possibilities! Engage the head center (logic) when it comes to what you're worried about. When you notice yourself holding on to hard feelings or fears around trust, walk yourself through a what if exercise:

What if they don't trust me right away? (Work on strengthening the relationship for stronger partnership in the future.)

What if they don't like me? (They aren't your people, and that's OK! Not everyone will be.)

This will help you change your mindset from viewing it as an attack to viewing it as an opportunity.

If you are feeling attacked, and taking things personally, that is a sign you are engaged in your stress type of 4: harboring negative emotions, always worrying you're being judged. When you look toward opportunity and how the obstacle can be shifted positively, it indicates you are leaning into your health type of 7.

Now we can explore number two, how to use your core strengths to help you gain that trust you desire.

Use your core strengths to help grow trust by again, activating the 7 and exploring possibilities. Ask yourself, "what from my strengths would build trust with that client?" Some thoughts might be:

- *Outlining clear next steps*
- *Setting expectations up front*
- *Providing details*
- *Having a strong follow up*
- *Providing Guides/Tutorials*

Type 2
Katie Caspero
Founder of OT Graphically, Healthcare Research Graphic Designer

Katie came to me struggling with time management challenges and wanting to better understand how to charge for her worth. Here is an excerpt from our conversation.

As a 2 you like to be asked for help and are naturally giving of your time. This often leads to you taking on all of the projects, regardless if they're a good fit. You find value by helping and giving; a tendency that consequently makes it difficult to know when to ask for help. Because of that you end up having a really full plate! In addition to having a full plate, you really do enjoy helping people, so it's hard for you to charge your worth because you're so in touch with what others want and need, you forget about what what you want or need.

To help combat these things there are a few key questions to ask yourself daily:

1: What is mine to do and why would I want to do this?
- *You can't do everything you may want to do, but you can do everything you can within your time boundaries. You don't have to have an immediate answer to clients. Give yourself permission to take time to pause. Consider whether you are doing it because you need to feel loved and appreciated by others, or because you actually want to.*

2: What are my needs?
- *Really get in touch with your core needs by listing them out and posting them where they can serve as a reminder. When it comes to setting your fees, think about these needs first and your client's needs second. If you continue to say yes to everything and repress your needs, you will become resentful quickly. Becoming resentful in your work has a lot to do with not asking for help, and not understanding when to say no.*

Type 3
Chelsea Goodwin
Co-Founder/CEO of The Agent Accelerator

Chelsea came to me with the obstacle of wanting to feel and be more authentic. When talking about this obstacle Chelsea said:

"I find it hard to be myself when I meet someone in business, whether it's a sales lead, potential partner, investor, or new employee, I zero in on how that person needs me to be and can easily mirror and match to them that means I'm not being authentic and it's harder for me to build close relationships with people. I always need to be "on".

Here is an excerpt from our conversation and how I coached her through this.

"Type 3s are often perceived as insincere or even manipulative. But this obstacle is actually a superpower if used correctly.

Blending into the environment is actually the 3s coping mechanism. Type 3s are the chameleons of the Enneagram world. They can blend in or attach to whoever they are around to avoid failure.

Instead of looking at this as a negative, I want to encourage you to lean into your health type of a 6, that logic center, and ask yourself: "what if this was actually a good skill? What if by being able to zero in on what someone needs from me makes me better in my career? What if by easily mirroring someone's behavior allows them to feel safe when working with me?"

These skills of reading a room, feeling what someone needs, positioning yourself in a way that draws people to you, are all positive skills.

Where this becomes dangerous is if you're so concerned with getting the sale or feeling accepted, that you forget who you are.

It's important for 3s to check in with themselves by asking questions like:

Am I withholding information or not showing emotions because I'm afraid I will be negatively perceived?

Am I forming relationships because I want to, or because of the level of prestige it might give me?

It's also important to take time to explore inner thoughts and feelings to help you to be honest with yourself. Let yourself and others appreciate you for who you are, rather than for what you do."

Type 4
Art Ordonez
Coffee Shop Barista

Art came to me struggling with dealing with criticism in the workplace. Here is what he said about this obstacle, and how it effects his life.

"I struggle with handling criticism and taking things personally at work. It doesn't matter if it's from my boss or a co-worker. It's also harder to receive criticism from anybody I deem important. When I receive criticism I have a very visceral response. I'm getting better at handling that response, and I'm getting better

at understanding it, but it's absolutely still an obstacle I face. It could really range from something bigger like you forgot to do this part of the procedure or something small like you're wearing those pants today? There's a very real fear response. I will say I'm on the self-preservation 4 side, so when I'm met with situations that I feel a lot of distress in, I tend to turn inward. I feel like my reality is that there is something innately wrong with me. The rest of the world doesn't have this damage I have, and that criticism is pointing that out."

Here is a strategy I recommended for Art.

"This is a common obstacle for type 4s and one I coach on often. Type 4s are feelers, they are in the heart center.

People in the heart center have very strong feelings, and 4s often have the strongest feelings of them all. That is one of your biggest gifts, but it's also one of your biggest obstacles.

Dealing with criticism is an emotional pattern for you. A type 4's natural instinct is to think about the negative feeling and emotion first. You have lots of feelings and emotions and you actually do feel happiness just not as intense as you feel sadness, so the happiness goes away.

This will need to be a mindset shift for you. Bringing facts around those feelings. To help you see them for what they are objectively, instead of what you feel they are.

Start with that negative feeling first. Validate that feeling. Speak it out loud. I feel BLANK and that's a valid feeling.

After you've articulated the feeling and validated it, it's time to ask, "Is this something I'm just feeling, or is this a fact?"

You gave the example of a co-worker not liking the music you had playing in the coffee shop as a minor criticism that you took personally. So an example of how this would look in practice would be:

I feel like BLANK doesn't like me because of my music choice. That feeling is valid. But is it true that she doesn't like me?

It's now time to dispel that feeling with facts like this:

She doesn't not like me, she just didn't like my music. She doesn't not like me, she just told me what a wonderful manager I am. She doesn't not like me because BLANK.

This exercise will help you train your brain to see the positive in the situation.

You have the choice. Are you going to let that comment ruin your day or are you going to take that opportunity to overcome that negative feeling and move on? If you don't intentionally take the time to find the positive your brain is instantly going to stay in the negative.

Type 5
Laura D. Frerichs
Registered Nurse

Laura came to me struggling with being able to commit to something new within her job. Here is the example she gave on struggling to commit.

"I have identified that I would like to "relevel" at work in my yearly evaluation. Currently, I am a Level 2 RN and could "relevel" to a Level 3. This is a 5% pay increase and it requires me to take on projects within my unit in order to stay "leveled". This requires me to essentially open myself up as a nurse, talk about my career, and why I believe I deserve to be recognized as a Level 3. It requires me to write an essay about my career and how I embody the spirit of an RN. This seems too invasive to me to expose myself and has thus prevented me from doing it so far."

Here was our conversation around that struggle.

"For true growth as a 5 you need to be able to do the following: connect to and express feelings as well as confront issues instead of isolating yourself and others from those feelings and issues. Essentially, you need to be able to turn your thoughts into action.

A type 5's energy is drained more easily than others when out of isolation so it's important that you take baby steps. You don't have to learn everything at once.

First we are going to talk about connecting with your health type of a 8 and getting into your body and understanding what you want. Begin with asking "why?"

Why would I want to relevel? You mentioned it's a pay increase. But what are the other benefits? Consider the other projects you would take on, would they stimulate your mind and make you feel more fulfilled?
Then ask yourself why you wouldn't want to relevel. Answering these questions will allow you to connect with and express your thoughts, so you can then confront them.

Once you have addressed some of those issues, write out the thoughts and try to identify the associated feelings. You can use this as an example:

Thought: I have to open up about myself.
Feeling Associated: Invasion of privacy

The third and final step is confronting the feeling. Start by asking yourself why it feels invasive. Consider if you are sitting in your core fear of feeling incompetent for the job, or maybe it is due to lacking the knowledge needed to get to that level three promotion. I recommend the use a journal to get these thoughts on paper.

This strategy of connecting with thoughts, expressing feelings and confronting the why, is the key for your success."

Type 6
Kristie Kinley
COO for Marketing Agency

One of Kristie's top obstacles at work is the challenge of taking on too much responsibility. When asked to go deeper into this obstacle, here is what she said.

"I tend to take responsibility over everything around me. Like it's all mine, it's all mine to do. I have a really hard time letting others take responsibility for what is actually theirs. I can not let things go. I have this irrational thought that I can impact or control everything, even though I know I can't. For example, since I'm the COO and over every department I feel responsible if something is not right in every part of the company. Maybe one sector of our company is just not operating at all cylinders or maybe somebody

is struggling on the team. I feel like it's my job to take on the responsibility of fixing it. I immediately think, what did I do wrong for this result happen. Every single time when something is off pace or we don't meet a goal, I feel like it's my fault, and I end up taking on more responsibility. That's when anxiety really comes into play. I start to spiral and really head to my type 3 stress point and start thinking about what I can produce to make this right. I get really task focused and start doing dumb things that make me feel productive versus really addressing the larger problem."

Here was how I coached Kristie through this obstacle during our conversation.

"One of the number one obstacles type 6's face is taking on too much responsibility. To help you feel more in control of the outcome and avoid you feeling like it's your fault, you take on more responsibility. This cycle happens with type 6s because they can sometimes struggle with empathy. That lack of empathy for themselves actually leads to mistrust, which is the core of why you take so much on.

When these thoughts and feelings of over-responsibility happen, for example, when you want to take over a project, this is when I really encourage sixes to engage their head center. Your brain is wired to fix things, so you being in this COO role is perfect. The growth pattern here is engaging that head center and beginning to ask yourself questions to help you discern what is yours to take on or what is someone else's to deal with themselves. I recommend What if questions like, what if I let someone on my team fail? What would be the worst thing that would happen?

Then you can go that step further. What if I let that person fail AND what if I could use my gifts to help them further themselves? Maybe you're at a point when answering these questions you can only think of a negative outcome.

Then take it another step further.

Try to make the what if questions more personal. What if I only think about the potential negative effects, what am I going to miss out on in my development or what are they going to miss out on in theirs?

You taking over responsibility for people and things is going to do nothing for you but slow you down and do nothing for them because they're not growing through their failure."

To wrap up our conversation on this obstacle, Kristie said the following:

" I really have to be intentional about it being positive, so that's a really good, different lense to look through. I definitely struggle with letting others fail because I feel like the responsibility is mine to bear, that it's a direct reflection on me. But I know that as a leader, failing is where I've learned all my lessons. Why, as their leader, would I not want to guide them through their lessons? What if instead of taking on their responsibilities, I could be the person that catalysts healthy change for them.

Type 7
Walt Anderson
President/COO Refuge Coffee Co

Walt came to me struggling with building consistent team chemistry. Here is an excerpt from our conversation.

"Without your team, you don't have a business and as a type 7, team building is one of your top qualities as a leader.

Team building starts with setting the tone for your employees and not only talking about the positives of working with your company, but the challenges as well. Focusing on the positives is your inclination because it's what feels good to talk about, but in order to build a strong team, hires need to understand the ups and the downs.

Also, it's important to help the team understand who they are working for, not just what they are working for. Let them in on your strengths and obstacles as well as those of the other leaders.

You might say something like: the morale of the company is important to me but I also like to synthesize data, move quickly and thrive on innovation, which doesn't lend time for a lot of explanation or ability to hype you up. Focus is hard for me and as a result, I don't love routine. So when working with me you may experience frequent schedule changes, I might have a lot of things I'm juggling and tend to forget things once in a while. I'm aware of these things and am constantly trying to improve.

This not only sets the tone for working with you, but also opens up the conversation to talk about their strengths and obstacles.

The more understanding you have of each other the better and the stronger your team will be. Therefore, this should be a continual conversation, not just a "one and done." Building team chemistry means keeping the door open. You might consider monthly or quarterly team building meetings.

You could start the meetings with a recap of business growth and strategies as well as how you are moving the mission forward with those strategies. Again, helping the team to see both sides of the company- the good and the challenging.

Type 7s are natural doers and don't often feel as though they have time to explain. Combat this by leaning into the health type of a 5 and using it to dig deep into the mission of the business. It will not only help you, but will strengthen your team.

During these meetings, Open the floor. Ask the employees what they think worked well and what didn't. Your brain does really well with data, so it would also help to ask your employees to gather data to support their responses. This not only helps you to feel good, but also to bring the team together.

Type 8
Brittany Fitzgerald
Owner of Infinity Family Services
Childbirth and Family Life Educator, Postpartum Practitioner and Motherhood Mentor

Brittany came to me struggling to take care of the detailsand administrative parts of projects she works on within her business. However, when she does get sucked into the details, she feels like she can't stop and just let things be. Like most common obstacles within each type, this is definitely one that type 8s struggle with often. Here is what I coached Brittany through in our conversation.

"It sounds like with details you are either feast or famine and guess what, you're not alone! Due to the type 8s strengths of strategy and being extremely action oriented, small details often get overlooked or even sometimes intentionally ignored. To overcome this obstacle, a type 8 must be intentional about calling this behavior out when it arises. You may have thoughts pop up in your head like:

"Is this really going to move the dial?"
"Is this really the best use of my time?"
"Do these details really matter?"

On the flip side, a type 8 can get very into details or the nitty gritty of a project when they feel out of control or pressured. This happens because of the 8s need for control and independence around a project (or person).

When any of these thoughts or actions begin to happen, take that awareness and turn it into action. Stop what you're doing to evaluate what led or what is leading you this place.

Some good questions to ask yourself when you are in the famine part of this obstacle (not wanting to pay attention to any details) may be the following?
"What if by focusing on the details of this project, my message will be more clear to my audience and make a bigger impact?"

"What if by slowing down and paying attention to the details I can actually assert more control over the quality of the final project?"

Now for the flip side, when you are on the feast part of this obstacle (not able to pull yourself out of a project) here are some things to consider?

Why do I feel the need to assert more control over this part of the project? Was I emotionally triggered?

Why would I want to step away? What are the consequences to my mental, emotional and physical health if I don't?

As a type 8 you have the power to push through anything when you put your mind to it. This can be one of your biggest strengths, and your biggest weaknesses. Slowing down is the key for both your feast and famine tendencies.

To help with the slowing down and answering of these questions, I recommend connecting with your body prior. Some ways you can do this might be deep breathing, grounding exercises and/or yoga. Connecting with the body is very important to type 8s. As a body centered type, being in touch with the sensations throughout your body will help you take more effective and sustainable action."

Type 9
Katie Anderson
Human Resource Advisor in the Air National Gaurd, Co-Founder of Inclusion Culture, doTERRA Wellness Advocate

Katie came to me struggling with speaking up and standing up for herself. Here is an excerpt from our conversation.

"To get to the core of you not speaking up and/or sticking up for yourself (this is the what you are doing), we need to drill down into the why. Why do you feel like you can't stick up or speak up for yourself. What are those fears that are holding you back?

In order to fully overcome this obstacle you have to call out those stories in your head (your internal facts, negative self-talk) you tell yourself, and turn them into feelings you can validate then work through."

Here's Katie's Response

"What first comes to mind is programming all throughout my life. Based on my childhood, my career in the military and I think a lot of the relationships in my past. I've journaled a lot about trying to figure out the root cause of confidence and I'm still kind of working through trying to figure it all out. Are there little things throughout my life that are just stories, like you suid, that I've played out so long and they're not even true. Is it just the emotion and feeling?"

"Would you say that maybe it's base on fear? Do you have a core fear of people misunderstanding you when you speak, or maybe you're scared if you speak up and share your opinion, it might

ruffle some feathers and that triggers your fear of conflict? Do you think that plays into any of that?"

"Absolutely. I love harmony. I don't really like conflict. I would rather just listen to somebody then do the talking, both because I'm more interested in other people and also it's a safer place for me to listen and ask questions. I take a little bit of time to mull things over and that's about honoring who I am."

"That's exactly right! The key for the type 9 is to be thoughtful instead of reactive. Being thoughtful is your essence. Being reactive is a trait that a 9 picks up in stress from the type 6.

Being reactive doesn't just mean exploding or saying something the second you think. Being reactive is making choice in the moment. It can even mean you seeing conflict brewing in a conversation and you making the choice to shut down, or not speak up.

When you are aware of your reactivity, you can shift back in the present and just be thoughtful of yourself (giving yourself empathy) in the moment.

Once you begin to practice empathy for yourself, you can begin to build confidence in who you are and your thoughts and opinions are valid. Then you can move to another why question, "Why would you want to speak up?"

Type 9s are body centered, meaning they make decisions and take action best by connecting with themselves and trusting their intuition. So when answering this question it's important to tap into your body. Think about how your body would feel if you spoke up? When you're doing this, you may also think about a time when you have spoken up and how it felt then, when you got a good result from sharing your thoughts.

Bring that memory and the feelings you're imagining when answering that question to the forefront of your body the next time you desire to speak up. This trains your brain that it's okay. Your fears are valid, but they can be overcome."

Throughout my research for this book I had several conversations I wish I could share, and maybe I will another time.

As we've come to the conclusion of this book I hope you've acquired the knowledge you need to help you Unlock Your Potential at Work. But what I truly desire is that you have learned things about yourself which you can not only incorporate in work, but in your personal life as well. Tapping into all the potential right inside of you. My desire is for you to have acquired more empathy for yourself and the people around you. *You* are the key to your success. It's time to take the awareness you have about your personality and turn it into action. It won't all come together right out of the gate, but I encourage you to continue to take the daily next best step in your path to success.

Appendix

Beck, Randall J., and Jim Harter. "Why Great Managers Are So Rare." *Gallup.com*, https://www.gallup.com/workplace/231593/why-great-managers-rare.aspx.

de Mol, Eva, et al. "What Makes Entrepreneurs Burn Out." *Hbr.org*, 10 Apr. 2018, https://hbr.org/2018/04/what-makes-entrepreneurs-burn-out.

Lapid-Bogda, Ginger, and Suenaon. *The Art of Typing: Powerful Tools for Enneagram Typing*. The Enneagram in Business Press, 2018.

Lapid-Bogda, Ginger. *Bringing out the Best in Everyone You Coach: Use the Enneagram System for Exceptional Results*. McGraw-Hill, 2010.

Rabha, Mrinmoy. "Employee Burnout: Understanding and Tackling It." *Vantage Circle*, 17 May 2021, https://blog.vantagecircle.com/employee-burnout/.

Smith, Melinda, et al. "Burnout Prevention and Treatment." *Helpguide.org*, Nov. 2021, https://www.helpguide.org/articles/stress/burnout-prevention-and-recovery.htm.

Tierney, John. "Do You Suffer From Decision Fatigue?" *NYTimes.com*, 17 Aug. 2011, https://www.nytimes.com/2011/08/21/magazine/do-you-suffer-from-decision-fatigue.html.

"What Are the Characteristics of a Good Leader?" *CCL.org*, 23 Aug. 2021, https://www.ccl.org/articles/leading-effectively-articles/characteristics-good-leader/.

About the Author

Hillarie Kay is an Enneagram Coach, Speaker and Trainer.

From business owners and startups to corporations and nonprofits, she helps her clients build sustainable business strategies using the Enneagram to reduce overwhelm, avoid burnout, and increase the quality of both internal and external communication.

When she's not coaching or training on the Enneagram, she spends time with her husband, two sons and three step-sons, splitting her time between Southeast Missouri and the Raleigh-Durham area of North Carolina.

She's obsessed with the 60s and you can often find her thrifting at antique shops and browsing record stores.